Musical Plays

BY

EILEEN DIAMOND

Editor: Robin Norman
Music and text setting: Crabtree Music, PO Box 484,
Bury St Edmunds, Suffolk, England
Vocals on recording: Helen Speirs and Jonathan Cohen
Pianist on recording: Jonathan Cohen
Recording engineer: John Drinkwater
Recorded at Cordrope Studios
Cover design: Glide Design

This edition published 2005

International MUSIC Publications

Musical Plays

Contents

Scripts *(These may be copied as required)*

Introduction

This new edition of Eileen Diamond's Musical Plays has been completely revised and amended by the composer and includes a CD recording with vocal and instrumental tracks of each play for demonstration and learning and also, on a second CD, backing tracks only of each play for use in performance, enabling children to sing and play the percussion parts themselves. The accompaniments have been recorded at a steady pace allowing time for children to manage their parts including actions and instruments unhurriedly and with ease.

The CDs provide an invaluable resource for teachers who do not play the piano as well as for musically trained teachers, leaving them free to direct and supervise the production.

These nine short, easy to produce, musical plays suitable for Key Stages 1 and 2 (children aged approximately 4 to 9 years) are stimulating and enjoyable to perform with humorous dialogue and catchy tunes.

While generally encouraging self-confidence, co-operation and working together, each play also has a theme which relates in some way to the teaching of Personal, Social, Health Education and Citizenship (PSHE), a prominent feature of today's education.

Clear indications and suggestions for props, costumes and actions are given.

At the back of the book you will find the printed scripts for each of the plays. These may be copied as required so each child can have their own copy.

The vocal and instrumental tracks on the CD are expertly performed by Jonathan Cohen and Helen Speirs, two musically talented and renowned presenters of children's television and radio shows.

As well as bringing these musical plays into the realm of non-musically trained teachers, the CDs also provide a most enjoyable experience of listening to musical stories for pre-school and primary school children both in the classroom and at home.

PSHE relevance

THE TOY SHOP
Good behaviour; how one's actions affect others.

THE LITTLE GINGERBREAD MAN
Feelings: sad; happy; worried; scared; excited.

THE SCARECROW
Looking after the environment. Caring for plants and crops.

THE SAD KING
Feelings. The needs of other people. Likes, dislikes. A duty of care.

THE TADPOLE and the CATERPILLAR
Differences and similarities between people/creatures. Bullying is wrong. Anti-social behaviour. Awe and wonder for the world we live in. Physical changes, e.g. growing up.

BIG CHIEF RED FEATHER
Fairness. Friendship. Right and wrong. Conflict and how to resolve it. Sharing. Being co-operative and working together.

THE PRINCESS WHO COULDN'T MAKE UP HER MIND
Consideration and feelings for others. Making decisions. Seeking advice, asking for help from family. Looking after living things e.g. plants.

THE SLEEPY MANDARIN
How one's actions affect others. Being responsible. Fairness.

A LITTLE MAGIC GOES A WRONG WAY
Medicines and products can be harmful if not handled properly. Following rules, rules help us. Being responsible. Seeking help. Feelings and needs of other people. Learning from mistakes.

The Toy Shop

Words and Music by
EILEEN DIAMOND

List of Characters

THE TOYMAKER
RAG DOLL
SOLDIER   } Solo parts
CLOWN
FAIRY DOLL

Other children may be dressed up as toys and join in the action.

CHORUS   Any number

Musical Instruments

CUCKOO CLOCK   C and A chime bars or metallophone
WHISTLE   Whistle or recorder
BELL   Hand bell
TELEPHONE   Rapidly played triangle

Props and Costumes

For the Toymaker: Nightshirt or pyjama top, slippers, work bag,
                  duvet or blanket and pillow for bed.
Appropriate clothes for the TOYS
Any children's toys to sit around the toy shop. A doll's tea set, conveniently placed. A screen would be effective to divide the TOYMAKER's bedroom from the shop, (but it is not essential).

The CHORUS stand backstage; in front of them to one side, stand the four musical instrument players; on the other side is the TOYMAKER's bed.

The TOYMAKER stands centre-stage with his bag open on the floor. The four TOYS sit on the floor in front of him. Other toys stand or sit nearby.

Action

The triangle player strikes six times. After a slight pause, the introduction begins and the CHORUS starts to sing. The TOYMAKER performs appropriate actions and waves to his toys as he says good-night. He moves over to his bedroom, takes off his slippers and lies down. When the whistle blows for the third time at the end of the chorus, the TOYMAKER sits up in bed and puts his hand to his ear to sing 'Did I hear a noise?' etc. At the words 'Oh, no', he shakes his head, makes hand actions pretending to turn out the light, waves good-night again to the toys and folds his arms firmly at the words, 'So it must be alright.' He lies down again. When the CHORUS sing 'But the toys had decided to play', the TOYS stand up and sing their parts. They form a line behind the SOLDIER and march around while the instruments play; they stand still when the CHORUS sing 'The toymaker said as he sat up in bed'.

The TOYMAKER sits up and makes the same hand actions as previously, before lying back on the bed again.

The CLOWN begins a polka at the words 'One, two and three, hop' and beckons to the other toys to join him. They all dance the polka while the instruments play; then they sit down on the floor.

Towards the end of the chorus, the TOYMAKER sits up listening, gets out of bed and kneels down with his ear to the ground. He stands up and repeats the previous actions. After the words 'But I think I'd better see', he puts on his slippers and begins moving towards the shop, timing his actions to arrive after the TOYS whisper good-night.

Meanwhile, the TOYS pretend to drink tea and perform the other actions. They whisper good-night to each other, close their eyes, and pretend to be asleep.

The TOYMAKER arrives centre-stage and sings his part 'Those noises I heard', etc.

The TOYS sit up and wink at each other, then stand up. The TOYMAKER moves towards them and they all dance freely to the final chorus.

PSHE Relevance

Good behaviour; how one's actions affect others.

The Toy Shop

Performance track 1
Backing track 1

Words and Music by
EILEEN DIAMOND

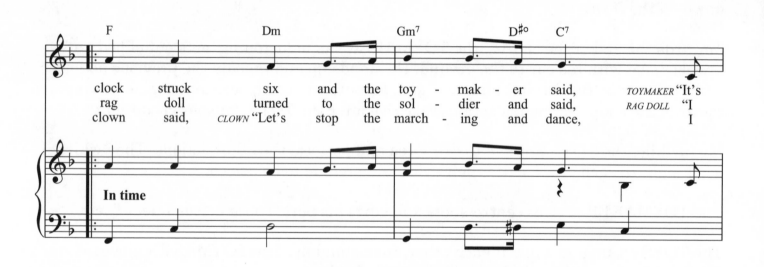

turned out the light
on while I lead."
ea - sy to do.

And he said to his toys good - night.
CHORUS And the o - ther toys all a - greed.
Come on try it and join in too."

TOYMAKER *(speaks):* "Good-night, toys." *(exits, waving)*
TOYS *(nodding agreement):* "Yes, we'll follow."
TOYS *(nodding to each other):* "Yes, come on!" *(They dance)*

CHORUS Then the cuck - oo sang in the

Chime bars

cuck - oo clock, And the whis - tle blew on the train, Then a

bell went clang, and a tel - e - phone rang, And the whis - tle blew a -

The Little Gingerbread Man

Words and Music by
EILEEN DIAMOND

List of Characters

CHEF   Solo part
1ST GINGERBREAD MAN ⎫
2ND GINGERBREAD MAN ⎬   Action only
3RD GINGERBREAD MAN ⎭
4TH GINGERBREAD MAN   Solo part
QUEEN   Solo part

CHORUS   Any number

Props and Clothes

A large picture of a gingerbread man which the CHORUS can point to when they sing:
"Then made a little man who looked like that".

A low table on which the CHEF can roll out his dough.

CHEF: A rolling pin, chef's hat and trousers, white shirt and apron.

QUEEN: a crown and appropriate dress.

4 GINGERBREAD MEN: beige or brown trousers and T shirts with 3 large 'Icing
buttons' made out of coloured sticky paper down the front. On top of this a 'Dough'
costume can be worn made from an old sheet cut into a loose shape (x2) and stitched
together down the sides, with a Velcro fastening down the back.

Action

The CHORUS stand around the back of the stage.
In front of them, the CHEF, holding a rolling-pin, stands behind the table.

The QUEEN waits off-stage.

Four children crouch down beside the CHEF. They are the 'pieces of dough' to become
the four GINGERBREAD MEN.

As the music starts, the CHEF takes the first piece of dough – this child lies on the table
– and pretends to roll it with the rolling pin.

The CHORUS point to mouth, eyes, arms, legs etc. as they sing about them. When the CHEF has rolled the dough, he helps the child off the table and removes the top costume, revealing the little gingerbread man underneath. At the words, 'He's a lovely little gingerbread man', the CHEF and the 1ST GINGERBREAD MAN dance together. Then the 1ST GINGERBREAN MAN stands to one side and the CHEF repeats the actions with the 2ND and 3RD pieces of dough, during the second and third verses.

The fourth verse is then enacted. At the words, 'He made one, two, three', the 4TH GINGERBREAD MAN (the remaining piece of dough) points sadly to the other three GINGERBREAD MEN and at the end of his solo, crouches down once more.

The QUEEN enters and sings her part to the CHEF. When she has finished, on the cue "There now are four" the 4TH GINGERBREAD MAN pops up to sing: "What was that I heard, upon my word!" and crouches down again.

The CHEF makes the 4TH GINGERBREAD MAN, and is then joined by the QUEEN and all four GINGERBREAD MEN for a final dance.

PSHE relevance

Feelings: sad; happy; worried; scared; excited.

The Little Gingerbread Man

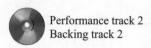

Performance track 2
Backing track 2

Words and Music
EILEEN DIAMOND

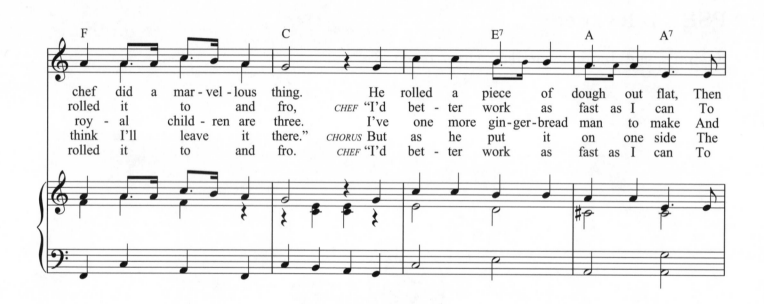

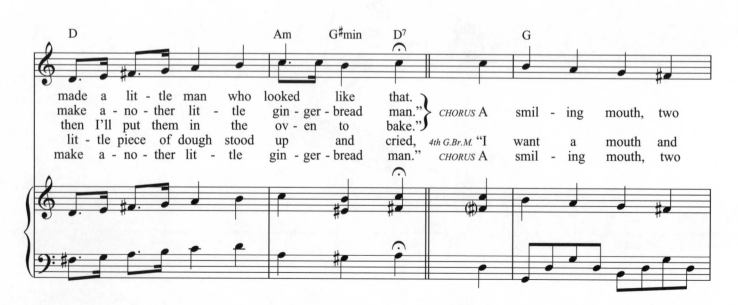

to Coda last time ⊕

1.2.3 **4.**

C · D⁷ · G⁷ · C

all things nice. He's a love - ly lit - tle gin - ger - bread man. 2. The man." *CHORUS* 5. The
did - n't need me, And I want to be a gin - ger - bread 3. The
all things nice. He's a love - ly lit - tle gin - ger - bread 4. The

C · F · C

Queen came and told the chef, *QUEEN* "I see the child - ren have a friend for tea So what

E⁷ · A · A⁷ · D · Am G♯min D⁷

e - ver you're mak - ing you will need one more. In - stead of on - ly three, there now are four."

Dmin · D⁷ · Dmin D⁷ · A⁷ D⁷ · G · **D𝄋 al Coda** · ⊕ **CODA**

C

4th G.Br.M. "What was that I heard? Up - on my word!" *CHORUS* 6. So the man.

The Scarecrow

Words and Music by
EILEEN DIAMOND

List of Characters

FARMER
WIFE
4 CROWS   Solo parts
WATCHMAN
SCARECROW

CHORUS   Any number

Props and Costumes

A large plastic sheet
1 chair (for Watchman)
A large empty pot with the word GLUE painted on in large letters
3 or 4 large sticks
1 pair of binoculars
For the Crows: black leotards and tights
For the Farmer: jeans and a shirt
For the Wife: jeans and shirt or a skirt or dress and a handkerchief
For the Scarecrow: An old hat with bits of straw sticking out; a
                    raggedy patched jacket and trousers and shirt

Action

The FARMER and WIFE act feeding the animals and scattering seeds. Then they lie down and 'fall asleep'. The CROWS fly in, swoop down to ground and fly off again.

The FARMER and WIFE wake up and sing "Oh dear our crops" etc. They fetch the plastic sheet, stretch it out, lay it on the ground and pretend to fix it with a hammering action. They 'fall asleep' again after "Yes that was a good idea".

One person from the CHORUS steps forward to lift the sheet and whisk it away off stage like a sail.

The FARMER and WIFE wake up and sing "Oh dear our crops" etc. The WATCHMAN enters running. He peers through his binoculars, sits on the chair and sings his part. All three 'fall asleep'. The 4 CROWS fly in as before, swoop and exit.

The FARMER and WIFE wake up. The WIFE takes out her handkerchief and 'weeps' while singing "'Oh dear our crops" etc. The FARMER fetches the SCARECROW'S clothing, sticks and glue pot and sets them down on the stage. The WATCHMAN exits.

The WIFE brings on the SCARECROW and she and the FARMER dress him in the jacket and hat and lift his arms at the appropriate words and pretend to paint his face etc. The SCARECROW stands there and moves his arms at the words "One arm like this and the other like that." He sings " Nobody will come near me".

The CROWS fly in and sing their parts. The 1ST CROW points to the SCARECROW; all four CROWS look very scared. They fly away and everyone joins in singing the last chorus.

PSHE relevance

Looking after the environment. Caring for plants and crops.

The Scarecrow

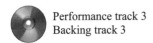

Performance track 3
Backing track 3

Words and Music by
EILEEN DIAMOND

then they left him stand - ing there. With his

SCARE-CROW "No - bo - dy will come near me." *CHORUS* The

next day when_ the crows flew by_ they saw him stan - ding there,

CROWS quiet and scared

1st CROW "I

A little slower

don't much like_ the look of him." _ *2nd CROW* "Oh dear," *3rd CROW* "Oh dear," *4th CROW* "Oh dear." *1st CROW* "I

think that he_ could do us harm." _ *2nd CROW* "Oh yes, I think so too." *3rd & 4th CROW* "We'd

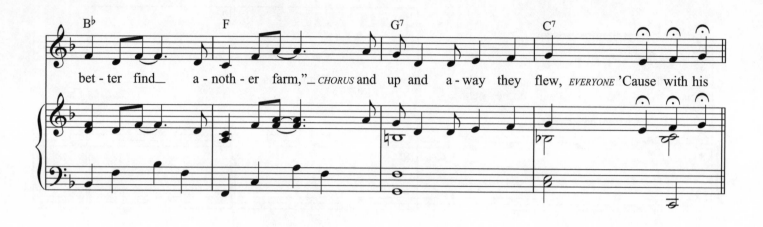

The Sad King

Words and Music by
EILEEN DIAMOND

List of Characters

KING
1ST GIRL
2ND GIRL   Solo parts
3RD GIRL
THREE COURTIERS   Action only

CHORUS   Any number

Props

Crown and cloak for KING.
Jewellery and pearls for 1ST GIRL.
Large 'Diamond' brooch for 2ND GIRL.
(This can be made out of cardboard, glue and silver glitter)
White 'wedding dress' and veil for 3RD GIRL.

The GIRLS wait off stage. CHORUS stand at back of the stage.
In front of them, the THREE COURTIERS stand to one side.

Action

While the CHORUS sing the first verse, the KING walks up and down centre stage. He looks very sad and makes occasional loud sighs.

At the words 'He sent all his courtiers' the KING beckons to the COURTIERS and points, directing them off stage. The COURTIERS exit and return with three GIRLS who curtsey to the KING and stand to one side. The COURTIERS move to the opposite side of the stage.

After the KING sings his solo 'I wonder why you yearn' etc., the 1ST GIRL steps forward and curtseys before singing her solo, pointing to the jewels. The KING sings again, and the 1ST GIRL returns to her place. The CHORUS sing and the KING walks and sighs as before.

The 2ND GIRL steps forward, curtseys before singing and points to large diamond brooch at appropriate words. She points her finger at the KING for 'I'd keep a strict eye on you', the KING reacts as for 1ST GIRL.

The 3RD GIRL steps forward and curtseys. The KING now looks very sad and keeps his head down until CHORUS sing 'The King raised his head'. He smiles, and holds out his hands. He sings 'Please marry me', the GIRL nods her head. They exit together.

The CHORUS sing 'Oh King' etc., during which the GIRL makes a quick change into her dress and veil. (The music slows down before the Wedding March to allow more time)

The KING and his Queen enter and walk round the stage hand in hand, they kiss centre stage and stand looking happy.

PSHE Relevance

Feelings. The needs of other people. Likes, dislikes. A duty of care. Social behaviour.

The Sad King

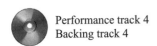

Performance track 4
Backing track 4

Words and Music by
EILEEN DIAMOND

Gently and not too fast

CHORUS The King walked a - lone in his pal - ace, he had
 sent all his cour - tiers out search - ing, they

ne - ver been so un - hap - py in his life, for al - though he was King, and
found the pret - ti - est girls to be seen, but the King had a task, each

he had ev - ery - thing, he just could - n't find him - self a wife.
girl he had to ask, to tell him why she want - ed to be Queen.

A little slower

The Tadpole and The Caterpillar

Words and Music by
EILEEN DIAMOND

List of Characters

NARRATOR   (This part may be shared by two children if wished)
TOBY TADPOLE   (a small child)
OTHER TADPOLES   (any number of larger children)
MOTHER FROG and FATHER FROG
TOBY FROG
BIRD
CHILDREN
MOTHER FISH and BABIES
CATERPILLAR
BUTTERFLY

Scenery and Props

Use a painted garden scene for the background.
The perimeter of the pond may be suggested by large toy building bricks or cardboard or egg boxes stapled or glued together to form a circle. For rocks, use painted paper attached to cardboard boxes for support.

Costumes

TADPOLES: Black tights and leotards.
BIRD, FISH AND CATERPILLAR: painted masks made out of stiff paper.
For the CATERPILLAR, a toy snake or draught excluder covered in green material and attached to the child's waist at back could make an effective tail.
BUTTERFLY: wings may be made from a length of white gauzy material (possibly an old curtain) with the centre stitched to the back of the child's clothing and two ends attached round elastic bracelets worn on the child's wrists.
FROGS: could wear a flat cap with a ping-pong ball on either side attached with velcro for the eyes. A sweater with a cushion stuffed underneath; tights and flippers for the feet.

Action

The NARRATOR remains on stage throughout.
While the Introductory Music is played, the TADPOLES move around inside the pond centre stage and MOTHER and FATHER FROG sit on the side by some rocks. They give one or two leaps when the NARRATOR mentions them.

At the end, after the FROG'S SONG, the whole cast enter and everybody sings the FINAL CHORUS.

PSHE relevance

Differences and similarities between people/creatures. Bullying is wrong. Anti-social behaviour. Awe and wonder for the world we live in. Physical changes e.g. growing up.

The Tadpole and the Caterpillar
Introductory and Interlude Music

Performance track 5
Backing track 5 & 10

Words and Music by
EILEEN DIAMOND

Very slow and tranquil

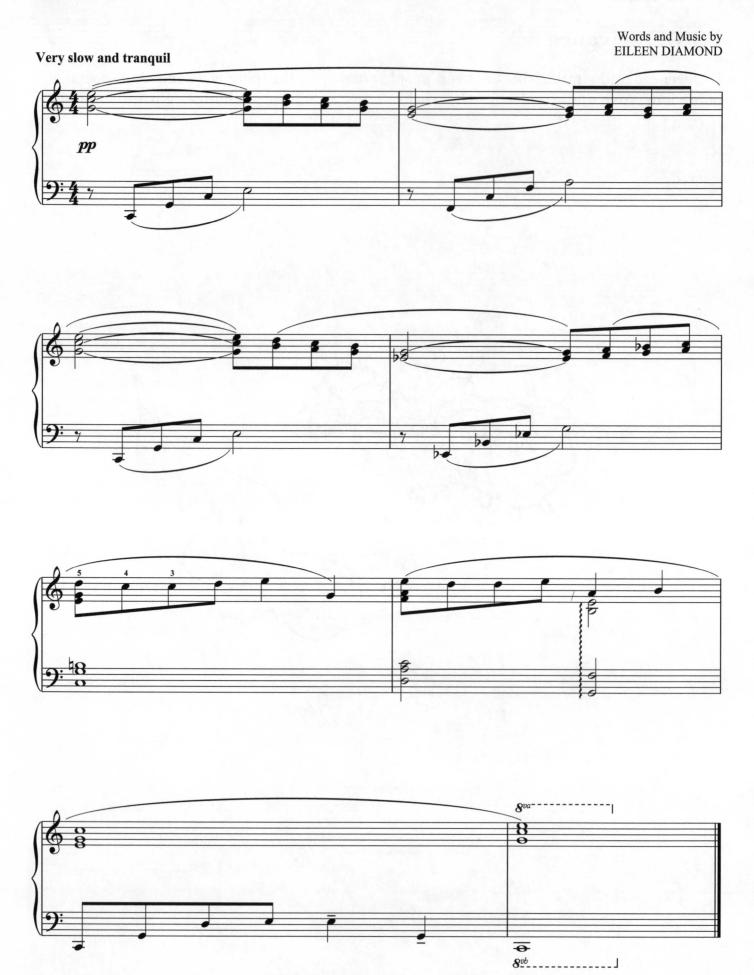

The Bird's, The Children's and
The Caterpillar's Song

Mother Fish and Babies' Song

Backing track 8

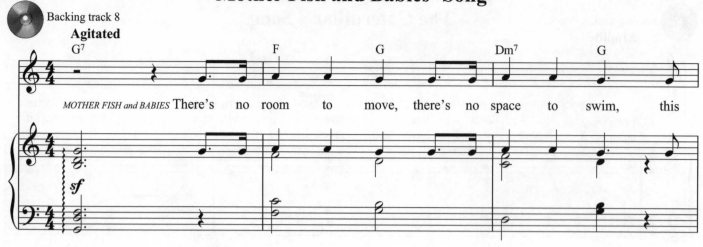

MOTHER FISH and BABIES There's no room to move, there's no space to swim, this

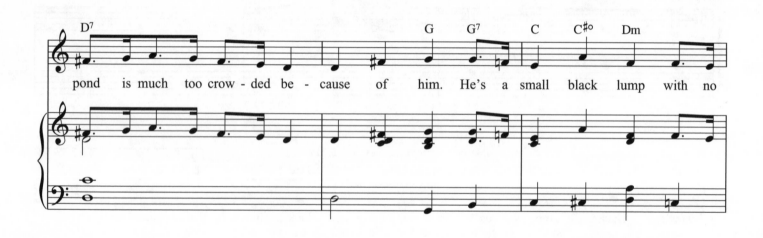

pond is much too crow-ded be-cause of him. He's a small black lump with no

legs to jump, he'll ne-ver e-ver be a frog!

The Frog's Song and Final Chorus

Big Chief Red Feather

Words and Music by
EILEEN DIAMOND

List of Characters

BIG CHIEF RED FEATHER   Solo part
NARRATOR   Solo part
RED FEATHER BRAVES
WHITE FEATHER BRAVES   Any number
SQUAWS

Musical Instruments   *Abbreviations*

Cymbal with beater   *Cym*
Tambourine   *Tb*
Triangle   *Tgl*
Wood-block or metronome (set on 66)   *W. Block or Metro*
Tom-toms.   *T-T*
There are two different rhythms for the tom-toms

| ♩ ♩ ♩ ♩ ‖ and | ♩ ♫ ♩ ♫ ‖

The children should practise both of them before performing for the first time, then ensure that they know when to play each one.

Props

Background painting of red Indian scene (tents, totem poles, mountains, etc.) One or two children's tents or tepees placed on stage if available.
Chair for Chief.
Small pile of firewood (red paper or card for flames).
Head bands and single red and white feathers for the two tribes (make from stiff paper).
Long feathered head-dress for Chief.
Bows, arrows and spears for Braves (use wire coat hangers, cardboard or wood).
An appropriate toy animal may be used for the 'Beast' or it could be made from material, sewn and stuffed.

Action

Firewood is scattered to one side of the stage, where a group of SQUAWS are sitting on the ground (with instruments).

BIG CHIEF RED FEATHER stands opposite, with arms folded, in front of the chair.

Where indicated in the first chorus, the RED FEATHER BRAVES enter in a line dancing and forming a circle centre stage. Excepting the CHIEF, all sing the main chorus, and on the word 'hail' raise their right hands (not the instrumentalists!). the CHIEF sings and everyone stands still. When the chorus is repeated the BRAVES dance round again (this action is consistent throughout).

The BRAVES exit, and the SQUAWS gather wood and prepare the fire. The CHIEF sits in his chair, the NARRATOR enters and stands to one side.

After 'Looking all around' the wood block player makes 'tick-tock' sounds continuing through the CHIEF'S speech, stopping on…'go and see.' Alternatively, the metronome is set as indicated on the text.

The CHIEF exits hurriedly and after the chorus the 'Beast' is brought in and placed on the ground by two BRAVES. The RED and WHITE BRAVES enter fighting. The CHIEF enters and stands looking angry.

The NARRATOR points to the beast and the fighting subsides. Both sides point to the beast as they sing. At the word 'STOP', the CHIEF raises his hand high.

When the chorus is repeated the 'Beast' is removed by two BRAVES, one from each tribe and both tribes dance and exit, led by the CHIEF, and enter again for the final dance chorus. The 'Beast' is laid in front of the fire.

PSHE relevance

Fairness. Friendship. Right and wrong. Conflict and how to resolve it. Sharing. Being co-operative and working together.

Big Chief Red Feather

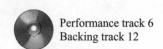

Performance track 6
Backing track 12

Words and Music by
EILEEN DIAMOND

Moderately

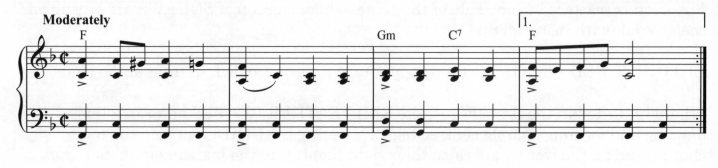

SQUAWS We will

(2nd time BRAVES enter dancing)

sing   the   tale   of   an   In - di - an   Chief,   an   In - di - an   Chief,   an
Chief   of   the   Red   Fea - ther   In - di - an   Tribe,   the   In - di - an   Tribe,   the

In - di - an   Chief.   We   will   sing   the   tale   of   an   In - di - an   Chief   who
In - di - an   Tribe.   He   was   Chief   of   the   Red   Fea - ther   In - di - an   Tribe   who

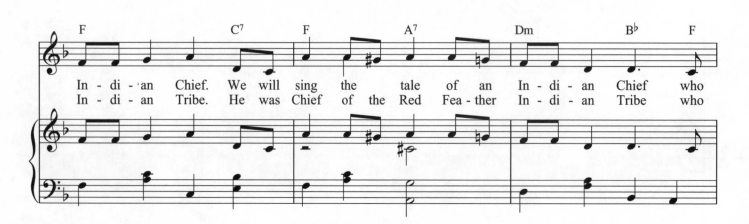

48

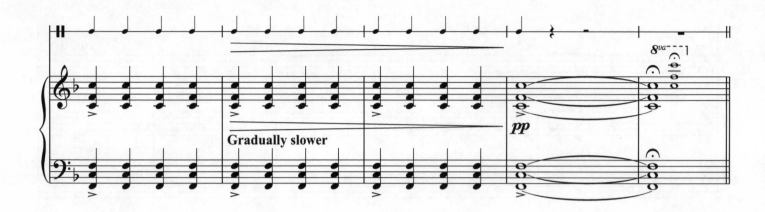

NARRATOR (spoken rhythmically)

So the tribe went off and the Squaws prepared
For the feast they would have that night.
They gathered up wood and piled it high
Ready to be set alight.
Then the Chief listened out for the tom-tom beat
But he could not hear a sound,
And he moved uneasily in his seat –
Looking all around.

(Metronome set on 66 or wood block: ♩ ♩ ♩ ♩ *etc.)*

As the hours ticked past he said.....

CHIEF

"Where can they be?
Why haven't they come back to me?
Perhaps they are in difficulty –
I think I'd better * go and see."

(Stop metronome or wood block)

Red Fea - ther, Red Fea - ther, brave and wise was he.

The Beast is brought in and placed on the ground.

Off went Big Chief Red Fea -ther, Red Fea - ther, ve - ry hur -ried - ly.

RED and WHITE BRAVES enter fighting.

NARRATOR When he found his tribe they were fighting with a tribe wearing feathers of white.

And the beast for the feast, lying on the ground, was the reason for the....

....fight. *RED BRAVES* "It be - longs to the Red." *WHITE BRAVES* "It be - longs to the White." CHIEF "Now

Slow and solemn

The Princess Who Couldn't Make Up Her Mind

Words and Music by
EILEEN DIAMOND

List of Characters

PRINCESS
KING
1ST PRINCE
2ND PRINCE   Solo singing parts
3RD PRINCE
NARRATOR   Solo speaking part

CHORUS   Any number

Props

Large written sign: THREE WEEKS LATER
Three empty flower pots
Bottle for perfume
Beads for jewellery
Crumpled black paper or earth to fill third pot
(The seed may be imaginary, or use large bead or fruit stone)
3 pieces of material to cover pots when filled
The CHORUS stand around the back of the stage. In front of them, the three PRINCES stand on one side, the PRINCESS stands central stage and the KING on the other side. The NARRATOR waits off stage, or may be one of the CHORUS.

Action

As the PRINCES sing "Oh I am hoping" etc. each one in turn takes a step forward. The PRINCESS steps forward to sing "Oh dear, oh dear" etc., putting a hand up to her head to express bewilderment. During the dance interludes between the verses, the PRINCESS takes the hands of each PRINCE in turn and dances once with each one, then moves over to the KING. The NARRATOR walks to front central stage speaks his part and exits.
The KING fetches three pots and gives one to each PRINCE, then points to off-stage dismissing the three PRINCES who exit. NARRATOR returns holding up THREE WEEKS LATER sign and exits.
The PRINCES return with their pots appropriately filled, each one covered with a piece of material. Each PRINCE uncovers his pot when he sings "See what I have here". The

pots are placed on the floor while the PRINCES dance. For the final dance, the PRINCESS dances only with the 3RD PRINCE.

PSHE relevance

Consideration and feelings for others. Making decisions. Seeking advice, asking for help from family. Looking after living things e.g. plants.

The Princess Who Couldn't Make Up Her Mind

Performance track 7
Backing track 14

Words and Music by
EILEEN DIAMOND

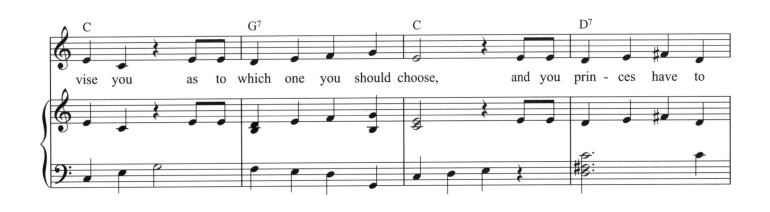

vise you as to which one you should choose, and you prin-ces have to

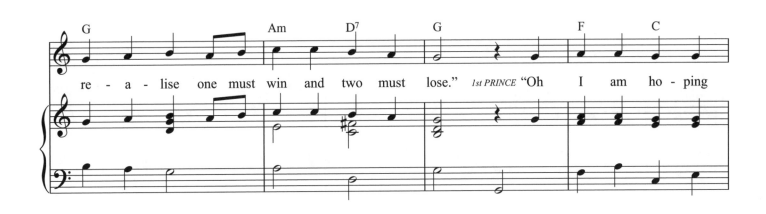

re-a-lise one must win and two must lose." *1st PRINCE* "Oh I am ho-ping

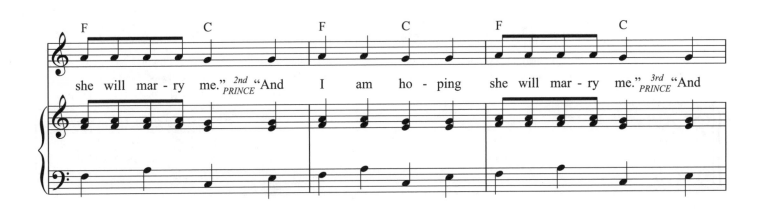

she will mar-ry me." *2nd PRINCE* "And I am ho-ping she will mar-ry me." *3rd PRINCE* "And

I am ho-ping she will mar-ry me." *PRINCESS* "Oh dear oh dear! Now

58

which one shall it be?" She just could-n't make up her mind. *(Dance)*

A little slower   **In time**

NARRATOR: The king then gave each prince an empty pot.

He told the princes to go away and fill their pots with something that they thought would most please the princess, and to return and present it to her three weeks later.

Exit NARRATOR and PRINCES

Backing track 15

NARRATOR enters & shows sign, then exits.
Enter PRINCES

1st PRINCE "Oh   prin - cess   dear   see   what   I   have   here,   all   my
prin - cess   dear   see   what   I   have   here,   prec - ious

Slowly   **In time**

The Sleepy Mandarin

Words and Music by
EILEEN DIAMOND

List of Characters

MANDARIN
4 AMBASSADORS ⎫ Solo singing parts
GIRL ⎭

4 SERVANTS

THE 'SOUND PLAYERS' (These parts may be doubled)
Drums ⎫
Bells ⎬ Any number of each
Claves ⎭

CHORUS ⎫ Any number
CITIZENS ⎭

Musical instruments

GONG (Cymbal with beater)   INDIAN BELLS (small finger cymbals)
TRIANGLE   SLEIGH BELLS
DRUMS   CLAVES

Props

Chair for the MANDARIN
Four pocket watches for the AMBASSADORS. (May be made out of cardboard hung on gold ribbon).

Two banners with large written letters, the first one saying:
**COMPETITION
BRING A SOUND TO WAKE THE MANDARIN**
The second one saying:

8 a.m. AT THE PALACE

Costumes

The AMBASSADORS should wear coloured sashes. Chinese style costumes and make-up for all other characters.

Action

The MANDARIN stands in front of a chair on one side of the stage attended by the SERVANTS (two on either side). Next to them stand the TRIANGLE, GONG and SLEIGH BELL PLAYERS. The CHORUS stand on the other side of the stage.

When the CHORUS start to sing, the CITIZENS enter and file past the MANDARIN, bowing to him. He shakes hands with them and appears to counsel them, after which they exit and the MANDARIN sits down. At the words 'But the Mandarin had a problem too' he 'falls asleep' and appears to be sleeping heavily (breathes deeply).

While the CHORUS sing, 'He was late' etc., the SERVANTS (gently!) shake him and try unsuccessfully to wake him. They sing 'Please will you wake up' urgently in his ears. The MANDARIN wakes up rubbing his eyes, stands to sing his part, then sits down and falls asleep again while the CHORUS sing 'He was late'.

When the AMBASSADORS enter they look annoyed, and constantly look at their watches. After singing their parts they exit.

The SERVANTS sing 'Nicest possible sound', and also exit. They return holding the banners, walking round with them while singing. They exit again and return without the banners to stand either side of the sleeping MANDARIN. The 'SOUND PLAYERS' and GIRL enter and stand centre stage. Each group in turn moves forward to play their 'Sound'. Before playing, one of the group conducts 4 beats to give the tempo.

The MANDARIN says 'That wouldn't get me out of bed' sleepily, dozes off again, and the 'SOUND PLAYERS' exit.

After the GIRL has sung her first refrain, the MANDARIN wakes and sits up listening interestedly, standing to sing 'That voice is much sweeter'. He falls asleep again after singing the words 'To get me out of bed'!

When the GIRL has sung her refrain, the AMBASSADORS again enter. The MANDARIN stands up and while the CHORUS sing, he greets the AMBASSADORS. During 'Has everybody heard?' the CITIZENS and 'SOUND PLAYERS' also enter. Everyone joins in the spoken words and sings the final chorus while the MANDARIN walks among them shaking hands. They bow as he passes.

Finally, he faces the GIRL, who bows to him: taking her hand, he bows to her.

PSHE Relevance

How one's actions affect others. Being responsible. Fairness.

The Sleepy Mandarin

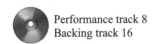

Performance track 8
Backing track 16

Words and Music by
EILEEN DIAMOND

Backing track 20

2nd time AMBASSADORS enter, MANDARIN gets up and greets them.

voice is much sweet - er than a bird, the love - li - est sound I
fol - low - ing morn at break of day, the Man - dar - in woke up

e - ver heard, so don't find an - y - thing else in - stead that's just what I need to
straight a - way, the girl would sing him the same re - frain, the Man - dar - in ne - ver was

1. get me out of bed." **2.** late a - gain. *AMBS.* "Has ev - ery - bo - dy
(loudly!)

Slower

Backing track 22

heard?" *(spoken)* *ALL* THE MAN - DAR - IN IS CURED! *AMBS.* "No long - er need we

A Little Magic Goes a Wrong Way

Words and music by
EILEEN DIAMOND

List of characters

WIZARD
ASSISTANT WIZARD
BOY   Solo parts
1ST LADY
2ND LADY

SMALL GIRL   Action only
CLIENTS IN WAITING ROOM } Any number
CHORUS

Musical Instruments   *Abbreviations*

Instrument	Abbreviation
Drum	*Dr*
Guiro	*Guiro*
Triangle	*Tgl*
Tambourine	*Tb*
Cymbals (beater)	*Cym*
Wood block	*W. block*
Shakers (any number)	*Shakers*

Props and Costumes

Bottles, storage jars, books, bowls and cooking spoon etc. (See scenery)
A black top hat. This can be made from cardboard/stiff paper and should be large enough to hold a toy rabbit.
A baby doll wrapped in a shawl or blanket.
Three 'spots' of different sizes, small, medium and large, made from red sticky paper for the 2ND LADY to stick on her nose.
Two long black cloaks and conical hats for the WIZARDS. These should be decorated traditionally with half-moons and stars. The ASSISTANT'S hat has an 'L' plate front and back. Two magic wands.

A large board covered with a poster on which the words 'THE END' are printed in very large letters. This should be covered by another poster on which there is a painting of a black cat. (A child can paint this). The cat poster could be stapled or attached with Velcro along the top to the underneath one so that at the end it can be folded back or pulled off by the ASSISTANT to reveal the words 'THE END'.

Scenery

Rows of chairs are placed on stage RIGHT, forming the 'Waiting Room'. The remainder of the stage represents the WIZARD'S room, with an imaginary door in between the two. Shelves and tables in the background exhibit a large array of bottles and storage jars filled with brightly coloured liquids and crystals (eg. Washing soda). Large labels on the jars read: MAGIC BREWS, LOTIONS, POTIONS etc. Several large books are also on view with such titles as: 'MAGIC SPELLS', 'DICTIONARY OF MAGIC', 'ENCYCLOPAEDIA OF WIZARDRY' etc. to the left of the stage is the WIZARD'S mixing table with bowls, cooking spoons and any other apparatus, together with the top hat containing a toy rabbit.

At one side of the stage is the board with the posters attached to it. This could rest on an easel if available, otherwise it could be propped up on a chair.

Action

The CHORUS and INSTRUMENTALISTS stand across the back of the stage between the two 'rooms'. The WIZARD'S clients wait off-stage right. The CHORUS sings the opening verses while the WIZARD busies himself in his room mixing brews, consulting his books etc.

At the words: 'Set up a waiting room', the BOY, 1ST LADY holding a baby and 2ND LADY enter and sit in the front row of chairs. The 2ND LADY wears the smallest spot on her nose and has the other two ready in a pocket.

At the words: 'Because he had so much to do', the ASSISTANT enters holding two magic wands. He passes one to the WIZARD and joins in the Magic Song with him.

As the clock strikes four, the BOY gets up and goes and knocks on the imaginary door of the WIZARD'S room in time with the wood block. The ASSISTANT lets him in and closes the door. After the BOY'S solo, the WIZARD takes the top hat, sings the Magical Song and on the final 'swish' produces the rabbit from the hat. The BOY thanks the WIZARD and exits holding the rabbit.

The 1ST LADY then knocks and is let in by the ASSISTANT. She sings her song and shows her baby to the WIZARD. The ASSISTANT then takes the baby and holds it in front of the WIZARD who waves his wand over it while singing 'Swish, swish, swish'. He then goes to his table and mixes something in the bowl while he sings: I'll mix a magic spell' etc. The ASSISTANT meanwhile takes the baby off stage. The WIZARD then moves to centre stage and with his back to the audience, raises his cloak on either side to hide the entrance of the ASSISTANT who is holding the hand of a small girl. On the final 'swish', the WIZARD drops the sides of his cloak to reveal them and the girl walks over to her mother. The 1ST LADY thanks the WIZARD and exits with her daughter.

After instructing the ASSISTANT to carry on, the WIZARD exits. The 2ND LADY goes and knocks on the door to be let in by the ASSISTANT. She sings her song and points to the spot on her nose. The ASSISTANT sings his version of the Magic Song and at the words: 'Swosh, swosh, swosh', he deliberately faces the LADY with his back to the audience. Hidden from view, the 2ND LADY sticks on the next size spot which the ASSISTANT steps aside to reveal. After 'No, that's not right' and during the

ASSISTANT'S speech, the 2ND LADY changes the spot again with the ASSISTANT this time facing the audience to hide her from view. He then steps aside and at the words: 'It's getting bigger', the 2ND LADY feels her nose, looking at the audience with great anguish!

When the ASSISTANT addresses the audience, he times his words according to their response. At the correct version of the Magic Song he again stands in front of the LADY. She removes her spot and he steps aside to reveal the success of his spell. After thanking him, the 2ND LADY exits.

The WIZARD enters. At the words: 'But here', the ASSISTANT points to the audience and at the final 'Swish' the WIZARD waves his wand towards the board. The ASSISTANT turns back the top poster to reveal 'THE END'.

The off-stage cast enter and everyone takes a bow.

PSHE relevance

Medicines and products can be harmful if not handled properly. Following rules, rules help us. Being responsible. Seeking help. Feelings and needs of other people. Learning from mistakes.

A Little Magic Goes a Wrong Way

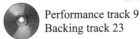

Performance track 9
Backing track 23

Words and Music by
EILEEN DIAMOND

won't take long when I sing this Mag - ic - al Song.

(spoken) Zip! Bang! Hul - la - ba - loo! Zip! Bang! Hul - la - ba - loo!

Swish! Swish! Swish!

Backing track 25

BOY: "Oh thank you Mister Wizard.
You really can do magical things.
I'm so pleased to have my rabbit back." *EXIT*

1st LADY knocks

1st LADY "Oh please Mis - ter

Zip! Bang! Hul - la - ba - loo! Zip! Bang! Hul - la - ba - loo!

(spoken)

Swish! Swish! Swish!

Backing track 26

1st LADY: "Oh Mister Wizard, what a clever magician you are. Thank you. I'll send all my friends to see you." *EXIT*

CHORUS Then one day when the

Slightly slower

Wiz - ard went to fetch a new in - gre - di - ent, he told his as - sis - tant

Backing track 27

ASSISTANT: *(Facing the audience and standing in front of LADY while she changes SPOT)*
"Oh dear, the Wizard will be angry if he comes back and finds I've done my spelling wrong. I just can't seem to remember the words of the Magical Song."
(ASSISTANT moves back to previous position)

2nd LADY: "I don't know what you're up to, Mister Wizard, but my spot hasn't gone yet. In fact, it feels as though it's getting bigger! Please can you hurry and make it disappear?"

ASSISTANT: (confused) "Oh, er...yes, ummmm... Well, the fact is, er...you see...
(suddenly confident) ..It has to get bigger before it's banished, But very soon now you will find it's vanished!"

 Backing track 28

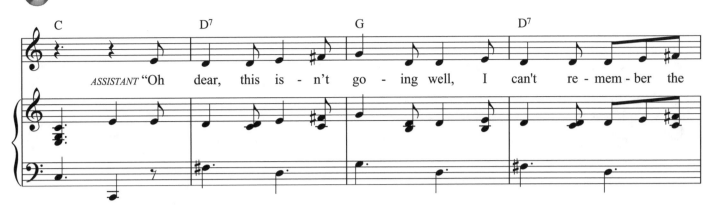

ASSISTANT "Oh dear, this is - n't go - ing well, I can't re - mem - ber the

mag - ic spell. I won - der if some - one here can tell? *TO AUDIENCE* Do you know the words of the

(spoken)

MAG - IC SPELL?"

(Waits for reply from Audience then:)
"What's that...? Will you say that
a little louder?" *(waits for response..)*
"Oh yes, NOW I remember..."

 Backing track 29

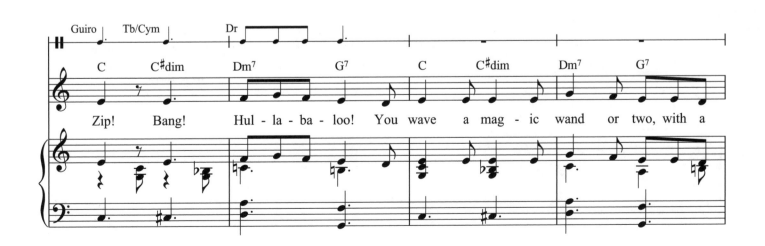

Zip!   Bang!   Hul - la - ba - loo!   You wave   a mag - ic wand   or two, with a

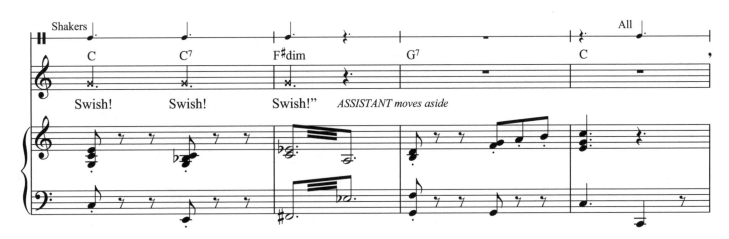

2nd LADY:
"Oh Mister Wizard, the spot's not there any more. It's completely gone!
Thank you very much, I shall always be grateful to you." *EXIT*

Backing track 30

ASSISTANT: *(to audience)*
"And I shall always be grateful to YOU!" *(Holds hand out towards audience)...*"Thank you."

The Toy Shop

Words and Music by
EILEEN DIAMOND

CHORUS   The clock struck six and the toymaker said:

TOYMAKER   "It's time now for me to go upstairs to bed."

CHORUS   He packed up his bag and he turned out the light
                And he said to his toys good-night.

TOYMAKER   "Good-night toys." *(exits waving)*
(speaks)

CHORUS   Then the cuckoo sang in the cuckoo clock,
                And the whistle blew on the train.
                Then a bell went clang
                And a telephone rang
                And the whistle blew again, again.
                Yes a bell went clang
                And a telephone rang
                And the whistle blew again.

                The toymaker said as he sat up in bed:

TOYMAKER   "Did I hear a noise? Could that be my toys?
                Oh no, it can't be, for I turned out the light
                And I wished them good-night,
                So it must be alright."

CHORUS   And upon his bed he lay,
                But the toys had decided to play.
                The rag doll turned to the soldier and said:

RAG DOLL   "I don't want to stay here all night in my bed."

SOLDIER   "Well let's take a march, follow on while I lead."

CHORUS   And the other toys all agreed.

TOYS *(speak, nodding agreement)*
                "Yes, we'll follow."

CHORUS | *Repeat Chorus:*
Then the cuckoo sang in the cuckoo clock, etc.

The toymaker said as he sat up in bed:

TOYMAKER | "Did I hear a noise? Could that be my toys?
Oh no, it can't be, for I turned out the light
And I wished them good-night,
So it must be alright."

CHORUS | And he lay back once again,
While the toys went on marching and then,
The clown said:

CLOWN | "Let's stop the marching and dance.
I wonder if you know the polka by chance?
It's one, two and three hop,
It's easy to do.
Come on try it and join in too."

TOYS *(speak, nodding to each other):*
"Yes, come on, let's try it!"

CHORUS | *Repeat chorus:*
Then the cuckoo sang in the cuckoo clock etc.

The toymaker said with his ear to the ground:

TOYMAKER | "I thought I could hear someone dancing around.
Oh no, it can't be for I turned out the light
And I wished them good-night,
So it must be alright.
But I think I'd better see."

CHORUS | Now the toys were all having some tea.

FAIRY DOLL | "This tea is delicious and so is the bread,
But someone is coming, quick, back into bed!"

CHORUS | They packed up the tea and they turned out the light,
And they whispered and waved good-night.

TOYS *(whisper good-night)*

CHORUS | The toymaker saw all his toys were in bed.

TOYMAKER | "Those noises I heard must have been in my head.
Perhaps I was dreaming, yes, that's what I think."

CHORUS

And the toys gave each other a great big wink.
Then the cuckoo sang in the cuckoo clock,
And the whistle blew on the train.
Then a bell went clang
And a telephone rang
And the whistle blew again, again.
Yes a bell went clang
And a telephone rang
And the whistle blew again.

The Little Gingerbread Man

Words and Music by
EILEEN DIAMOND

CHORUS

One day in the palace of the King
The chef did a marvellous thing.
He rolled a piece of dough out flat
Then made a little man who looked like that. *(Point to picture)*

A smiling mouth, two currant eyes,
The royal children will have a surprise.
Two arms, two legs and then the best,
Three icing buttons upon his chest.
He's a lovely little gingerbread man,
A lovely little gingerbread man,
Made of sugar and spice and all things nice.
He's a lovely little gingerbread man.

The chef took another piece of dough.
He rolled it to and fro.

CHEF

"I'd better work as fast as I can
To make another little gingerbread man."

Repeat chorus:
A smiling mouth, two currant eyes, etc.

The chef said:

CHEF

"Now then let me see,
The royal children are three.
I've one more gingerbread man to make
And then I'll put them in the oven to bake."

Repeat chorus:
A smiling mouth, two currant eyes, etc.

The chef had a piece of dough to spare.

CHEF

"I think I'll leave it there."

CHORUS

But as he put it on one side,
The little piece of dough stood up and cried.

DOUGH

"I want a mouth and currant eyes,
I want to be a nice surprise.
Two arms, two legs and then the best,
Three icing buttons upon my chest.
Oh I want to be a gingerbread man,
I want to be a gingerbread man.
He made one, two, three and he didn't need me
And I want to be a gingerbread man."

CHORUS

The Queen came and told the chef:

QUEEN

"I see the children have a friend for tea,
So whatever you're making you will need one more,
Instead of only three, there now are four."

DOUGH

"What was that I heard?
Upon my word!"

CHORUS

So the chef took the other piece of dough
And rolled it to and fro.

CHEF

"I'd better work as fast as I can
To make another little gingerbread man."

CHORUS

A smiling mouth, two currant eyes,
The royal children will have a surprise.
Two arms, two legs and then the best,
Three icing buttons upon his chest.
He's a lovely little gingerbread man,
A lovely little gingerbread man,
Made of sugar and spice and all things nice.
He's a lovely little gingerbread man.

The Scarecrow

Words and Music by
EILEEN DIAMOND

CHORUS

Oh there once was a farmer who worked very hard,
Feeding the animals in his farmyard
And he had a good wife would lend him a hand,
Sowing seeds upon the land.

But after they had worked all day
And fallen fast asleep,
Some crows flew in and stole away
The crops they hoped to reap.

FARMER

"Oh dear our crops have disappeared
Whatever can we do?"

WIFE

"I know, let's make a cover
Then they can grow anew."

CHORUS

They tool a large plastic sheet
And they stretched it out flat,
Fixed it like this and fixed it like that.

WIFE

"What a marvellous cover, the birds won't come near."

FARMER

"Yes that was a good idea!"

CHORUS

But when they fell asleep that night
There was a howling gale,
The wind blew underneath the sheet,
It took off like a sail!

FARMER

"Oh dear our crops have disappeared
Whatever can we do?"

WIFE

"I know, let's find a watchman
To watch the field for you."

CHORUS

They found a very strong watchman who knew how to run.
He sat in the field and said, "This will be fun;

WATCHMAN

If those birds come too near I will chase them and then,
They will not come back again."

CHORUS	But when night came and it was dark The watchman fell asleep; The crows flew in and stole the crop, The wife began to weep.
WIFE	"Oh dear our crops have disappeared Whatever can we do?"
FARMER	"I know, let's make a scarecrow With clothes and sticks and glue."
CHORUS	They found a raggedy coat and a raggedy hat, Put one arm like this and the other like that, Then they painted his face, put some straw for his hair, Then they left him standing there. With his raggedy coat and his raggedy hat, One arm like this and the other like that,
FARMER & WIFE }	"He's the scariest scarecrow you ever did see,"
SCARECROW	"Nobody will come near me."
CHORUS	The next day when the crows flew by They saw him standing there,
1ST CROW	"I don't much like the look of him"
2ND CROW	"Oh dear"
3RD CROW	"Oh dear"
4TH CROW	"Oh dear"
1ST CROW	"I think that he could do us harm."
2ND CROW	"Oh yes, I think so too."
3RD & 4TH CROWS	"We'd better find another farm,"
CHORUS	And up and away they flew.
EVERYONE	'Cause with his Raggedy coat and his raggedy hat, One arm like this and the other like that, He's the scariest scarecrow you ever did see,
SCARECROW	"Nobody will come near me."
EVERYONE	With his raggedy coat and his raggedy hat, One arm like this and the other like that, He's the scariest scarecrow you ever did see,
SCARECROW	"Nobody will come near me – no never! Nobody will come near me!"

The Sad King

Words and Music by
EILEEN DIAMOND

CHORUS

The King walked alone in his palace,
He had never been so unhappy in his life,
For although he was King, and he had everything,
He just couldn't find himself a wife.

Poor King, sad King,
He'd never been so unhappy in his life.
Poor King, sad unhappy King,
The only thing he wanted was a wife.

He sent all his courtiers out searching,
They found the prettiest girls to be seen,
But the King had a task, each girl he had to ask
To tell him why she wanted to be Queen.

Poor King, sad King,
He'd never been so unhappy in his life.
Poor King, sad unhappy King,
The only thing he wanted was a wife.

The King asked each in turn:

KING

"Please tell me why you yearn
To come and be my Queen and marry me?"
(1ST GIRL steps forward and curtseys)

1ST GIRL

"Oh I'd like to wear lots of jewellery
And I'd like to wear lots of pearls,
I'd so like to be very different you see
And not just like all other girls."

CHORUS

The King shook his head,
And this is what he said:

KING

"I'm very sorry dear but you won't do."
(1ST GIRL walks slowly back)

CHORUS

Poor King, sad King,
He'd never been so unhappy in his life.
Poor King, sad unhappy King,
The only thing he wanted was a wife.

2ND GIRL	"Oh I'd like to give lots of orders, And tell people what they have to do, I'd ride in your coach, wear a big diamond brooch, And I'd keep a strict eye on you!"
CHORUS	The King shook his head, And this is what he said:
KING	"I'm very sorry dear but you won't do." *(2ND GIRL walks slowly back)*
CHORUS	Poor King, sad King, He'd never been so unhappy in his life. Poor King, sad unhappy King, The only thing he wanted was a wife.
3RD GIRL	"Oh I'd like to visit the people, And help them as much as I can, But my main aim in life, is to be a better wife, And make you a very happy man."
CHORUS	The King raised his head, And this is what he said:
KING	"At last I've found true love, please marry me." *(KING takes 3RD GIRL by the hand and they exit)*
CHORUS	Oh King, happy happy King, At last he found the love he'd waited for. Oh King, happy happy King, He would not be unhappy anymore. *(KING and BRIDE enter after wedding march)* And then came the day they were married, The King took his bride by the hand, They kissed tenderly, and it was plain to see, He was the happiest man in all the land. Oh King, happy happy King, He'd never been so happy in his life. Oh King, happy happy King, At last he had found himself a wife.

The Tadpole and the Caterpillar

Words and Music by
EILEEN DIAMOND

INTRODUCTORY MUSIC

NARRATOR   Once upon a time, a tadpole swam in a pond in a garden. He was very small and black and it looked as though he was just a head stuck on to a tail. His name was Toby. He had lots of brothers and sisters who looked just like him and a mother and father who didn't look like him at all! In fact his parents were not called tadpoles, they were called frogs. Instead of tails they had legs, and went leaping about on the rocks which jutted out of the water.

Enter BIRD

NARRATOR   One day, a bird landed on one of the rocks near where Toby was swimming. He had an air of self-importance about him and seemed to look right down his beak at Toby.

TOBY   Good-morning.

BIRD   *(disdainfully)* Good gracious! Whatever are you?

TOBY   I'm a tadpole, my name is Toby,

BIRD   Well I've never seen the likes of you before! I've seen fish and frogs in all the other ponds I visit, but no little black lumps like you called – what did you say you were?

TOBY   A tadpole – at least for the present. One day I'll grow legs and turn into a frog.

BIRD   Hmph, like I'll grow scales and turn into a fish! Anyway, if you're going to be a frog, why aren't you called a *baby* frog now? You don't look anything like a frog to me; why, you're just a head stuck on to a tail.
(sings   You are thin and small
laughingly) Frogs are round and fat,
                    However are you going to look like that?
                    They have legs to jump,
                    You're a small black lump,
                    You'll never ever look like that!

TOBY   Oh dear.

BIRD flies away leaving behind a very sad looking tadpole.
A group of CHILDREN enter, one child points to the tadpoles.

1ST CHILD	See these tadpoles, one day they will change and grow into frogs.
2ND CHILD	That's impossible, they don't look anything like frogs.
TOBY	Oh dear, oh dear.
1ST CHILD	Look – and you will see, most of them have already started to grow legs; next they lose their tails, and then they become frogs.
TOBY	Oh, will that ever happen to me?
3RD CHILD	*(pointing at TOBY)* Well look at that one there, he's very small; he only looks like a head stuck on a tail and he has no legs.
4TH CHILD	No, he won't ever turn into a frog.
CHILDREN (sing)	What a tiny thing, He will not survive, It really is surprising he's still alive. He's a small black lump With no legs to jump, He'll never, ever be a frog!

CHILDREN laugh and run off;
TOBY looks very sad.
Exit other TADPOLES and FROGS.

NARRATOR	Toby was very sad. As he turned around in the pond he bumped smack into a goldfish swimming along with her babies.

Enter GOLDFISH and BABIES. TOBY and GOLDFISH bump into each other.

GOLDFISH	Hey! Can't you look where you're going? This pond is much too crowded these days, there's hardly enough room for me and my babies. Besides, you shouldn't still be swimming here, you should have legs by now and be jumping on the rocks, leaving us fish some space to move around. It's our pond you know. It's called 'The Fish Pond' not 'The Tadpole Pond.'
MOTHER FISH and BABIES *(sing angrily)*	There's no room to move, There's no space to swim, This pond is much too crowded Because of him. *(pointing to TOBY)* He's a small black lump With no legs to jump, He'll never ever be a frog!

FISH exit; TOBY sobs bitterly

NARRATOR	Poor Toby was sure now that he would never be a frog. He was so unhappy, he couldn't stop crying. Then it started to rain, and the pond became fuller and fuller. Onto one of the large flat lily leaves by the edge of the pond crawled a caterpillar.

Enter CATERPILLAR

CATERPILLAR	I say, do stop crying or you'll flood the whole garden, and I need to find somewhere peaceful where I can have my sleep before I turn into a butterfly.
NARRATOR	In his surprise at hearing the Caterpillar say this, Toby stopped crying immediately.
CATERPILLAR	What are you so sad about anyway?
NARRATOR	Then Toby explained how first the bird had scornfully told him he would never turn into a frog, how the children had said the same, and laughed at him, and finally how the fish had told him off for still being in the pond.
TOBY *(starting to cry)*	I don't know how I'll ever be a frog.
CATERPILLAR	Oh please, don't start crying again. You really don't need to worry. Nature never starts anything without finishing it, some things just take a little longer than others that's all. If I can change from a caterpillar into a butterfly, then there's no reason why you can't change from a tadpole into a frog.
TOBY	Did you say 'change from a caterpillar into a butterfly?'

CATERPILLAR *(reassuringly)*	Listen Toby:	
	(sings)	Though now I'm long and green I'll soon be white and flat, Perhaps you think I never will look like that. I'll have wings to fly, And not go crawling by. Yes one day I will look like that.
	(spoken)	And one day you *will* be a frog.

NARRATOR	Toby began to feel happier. Then suddenly he began to feel something else – sticking out from the back of his body he could feel two small legs.
CATERPILLAR	Look! Your legs have started to grow. I told you they would! *(he yawns)* I really am feeling sleepy. I think I'd better go. I'll come back and see you in a few months time Toby, but I won't be looking like this!
TOBY	And I won't be looking like this either. I know that now, thanks to you Caterpillar. Goodbye, have a good sleep.

Exit TOBY and CATERPILLAR

NARRATOR   It was some time later that a round plump frog jumped nimbly on to one of the rocks, and peered at his reflection in the water. Just then he saw another reflection. *(pause)* He knew who it was.

Enter BUTTERFLY and wait by the pond.

Enter TOBY FROG leaping in from opposite side.

BUTTERFLY   Hello Toby. What a very fine frog you have turned into.

TOBY   Thank you, and you are a beautiful butterfly. I know now that some things just take a little longer than others, that's all.
(sings   I'm not small and thin
happily)   I am round and fat,
             However did I manage to look like that?
             I have legs to jump
             I'm not a small black lump,
             Although it didn't happen fast –
             I really am a frog,
             I really am a frog,
             I really am a frog at last!

Enter WHOLE CAST

EVERYBODY   *(sings)*   He's not small and thin,
                         He is round and fat,
                         However did he manage to look like that?
                         He has legs to jump,
                         He's not a small black lump,
                         Although it didn't happen fast –
                         He really is a frog,
                         He really is a frog,
                         He really is a frog at last!

Big Chief Red Feather

Words and Music by
EILEEN DIAMOND

SQUAWS

We will sing the tale of an Indian Chief,
An Indian Chief, and Indian Chief.
We will sing the tale of an Indian Chief,
Who lived by a mountainside.

He was Chief of the Red Feather Indian Tribe,
He was Chief of the Red Feather Indian Tribe,
Who lived by a mountainside.

ALL

Hail to Big Chief Red Feather, Red Feather,
Brave and wise is he.
Hail to Big Chief Red Feather, Red Feather,
Happy may he be.
Oh! Hail to Big Chief Red Feather, Red Feather,
Brave and wise is he.
Hail to Big Chief Red Feather, Red Feather,
Happy may he be.

CHIEF to
BRAVES

"It is time to go out hunting.
Will you please bring back some meat?
If your hunting is successful,
On the tom-toms you must beat."

BRAVES

"We will do as you desire,
We will go and catch a beast.
Let the squaws prepare a fire,
Then tonight we'll have a feast."

CHIEF to
SQUAWS

"When you hear the tom-toms beat,
Light the fire and fan the heat."

SQUAWS

"We'll put on our best attire,
We will dance before the fire."

ALL	Oh! Hail to Big Chief Red Feather, Red Feather, Brave and wise is he. Hail to Big Chief Red Feather, Red Feather, Happy may he be. Oh! Hail to Big Chief Red Feather, Red Feather, Brave and wise is he. Hail to Big Chief Red Feather, Red Feather, Happy may he be.
NARRATOR *(spoken rhythmically)*	So the tribe went off and the Squaws prepared For the feast they would have that night. They gathered up wood and piled it high Ready to be set alight. Then the Chief listened out for the tom-tom beat But he could not hear a sound, And he moved uneasily in his seat – Looking all around. *(Wood block ♩ ♩ ♩ ♩ etc or start metronome on 66)* As the hours ticked past he said…
CHIEF	"Where can they be? Why haven't they come back to me? Perhaps they are in difficulty – I think I'd better go and see." *(Stop metronome or wood block)*
ALL	Off went Big Chief Red Feather, Red Feather, Brave and wise was he. Off went Big Chief Red Feather, Red Feather, Very hurriedly.
NARRATOR	When he found his tribe they were fighting With a tribe wearing feathers of white… And the beast for the feast, lying on the ground, Was the reason for the fight.
RED BRAVES	"It belongs to the Red."
WHITE BRAVES	"It belongs to the White."
CHIEF	"Now STOP! Both of you, this is not right. For the beast is large and we are few, There's enough for us and enough for you. So be our guests and beat your drum, The fire is ready so come, now come."

ALL Then the tribes put down their weapons of war,
And they raised hands peacefully.
They promised not to fight anymore,
Then sang out joyfully
Oh! Hail to Big Chief Red Feather, Red Feather,
Brave and wise is he.
Hail to Big Chief Red Feather, Red Feather,
Happy may he be.
Oh! Hail to Big Chief Red Feather, Red Feather,
Brave and wise is he.
Hail to Big Chief Red Feather, Red Feather,
Happy may he be.

Then they all went back to the Red Feather Camp,
The Red Feather Camp, the Red Feather Camp.
Then they all went back to the Red Feather Camp
Where they danced by the light of the fire.

And they beat on the tom-toms joyfully,
Joyfully, joyfully,
Then they beat on the tom-toms joyfully,
As they danced by the light of the fire.

Oh! Hail to Big Chief Red Feather, Red Feather,
Brave and wise is he.
Hail to Big Chief Red Feather, Red Feather,
Happy may he be.
Oh! Hail to Big Chief Red Feather, Red Feather,
Brave and wise is he.
Hail to Big Chief Red Feather, Red Feather,
Happy may he be.

Indian howls!

The Princess Who Couldn't Make Up Her Mind

Words and Music by
EILEEN DIAMOND

CHORUS	There was once a very pretty princess, She was fair and she was good. There were once three handsome princes, Who would marry her if they could.
1ST PRINCE	"Oh I am hoping she will marry me."
2ND PRINCE	"And I am hoping she will marry me."
3RD PRINCE	"And I am hoping she will marry me."
PRINCESS	"Oh dear oh dear! Now which one shall it be?"
CHORUS	She just couldn't make up her mind.
	(Dance)
CHORUS	So she went to ask her father Who was king of all the land,
PRINCESS	"Father please could you advise me To which prince shall I give my hand?"
1ST PRINCE	"Oh I am hoping she will marry me."
2ND PRINCE	"And I am hoping she will marry me."
3RD PRINCE	"And I am hoping she will marry me."
PRINCESS	"Oh dear oh dear! Now which one shall it be?"
CHORUS	She just couldn't make up her mind.
	(Dance)

KING

"Yes I think I can advise you
As to which one you should choose,
And you princes have to realise
One must win and two must lose."

1ST PRINCE

"Oh I am hoping she will marry me."

2ND PRINCE

"And I am hoping she will marry me."

3RD PRINCE

"And I am hoping she will marry me."

PRINCESS

"Oh dear oh dear! Now which one shall it be?"

CHORUS

She just couldn't make up her mind.

(Dance)

NARRATOR

The king then gave each prince an empty pot. He told the princes to go away and fill their pots with something that they thought would most please the princess, and to return and present it to her three weeks later. *(exit Princes)*

(Holds up sign saying THREE WEEKS LATER.
The Princes return with their pots)

1ST PRINCE

"Oh Princess dear see what I have here,
All my money I have spent
On something that I am sure you will like
It's a beautiful bottle of scent.
Oh I am hoping she will marry me."

2ND PRINCE

"And I am hoping she will marry me."

3RD PRINCE

"And I am hoping she will marry me."

PRINCESS

"I can't say now, you will have to wait and see."

CHORUS

She just hadn't made up her mind.

(Dance)

2ND PRINCE

"Oh Princess dear see what I have here,
Precious jewels of every kind,
Some sapphires blue and some diamonds too
This is sure to make up your mind."

1ST PRINCE	"Oh I am hoping she will marry me."
2ND PRINCE	"And I am hoping she will marry me."
3RD PRINCE	"And I am hoping she will marry me."
PRINCESS	"I can't say now, you will have to wait and see."
CHORUS	She just hadn't made up her mind.

(Dance)

3RD PRINCE
"Oh Princess dear see what I have here
I have filled my pot with earth."

1ST PRINCE *(horrified!)*
"With earth! What an insult!"

2ND PRINCE
"With earth! How does he dare!"

KING *(disbelieving)*
"Just earth! I can't believe it,
But wait! What does he have there?"

3RD PRINCE
"Now in this pot here's a seed I'll sow
Which is like my love for you,
For every day you can watch it grow,
It will give you pleasure too."

1ST PRINCE *(with dismay)*
"Oh dear" That's rather clever!"

2ND PRINCE
"I say! That's rather good."

KING
"Indeed, this man has something.
For the pot he has brought shows the greatest thought."

PRINCESS
"Oh yes, I agree, he's the prince for me."

CHORUS
She had suddenly made up her mind!

(Dance) – PRINCESS and 3RD PRINCE

The Sleepy Mandarin

Words and Music by
EILEEN DIAMOND

CHORUS

Very long ago in a far off land
Lived a Mandarin kind and good.
People came to him when they needed help,
He would do for them what he could.
But the Mandarin had a problem too
And nobody knew just what to do,
For every day though the clock would chime,
The Mandarin couldn't wake up in time,
Which meant he was always late!
Chorus
He was late, he was late, he was always late
Was the good and kindly Mandarin.
He was late, he was late, he was always late
Was the good and kindly man.

SERVANTS

"Please will you wake up, for the crowd outside
Now has grown to a multitude.
Please will you wake up, for to keep them waiting
Is really extremely rude."

CHORUS

The Mandarin woke up sleepily.

MANDARIN

"I wonder what can be wrong with me.
I need a sound that will make me wake,
So please will you find one for goodness' sake.
Only then will I not be late."

CHORUS

Repeat Chorus:
He was late, he was late etc.

1ST AMB.
"I've been waiting here since nine o'clock."

2ND AMB.
"And I've been here since eight."

Both AMBS.
(angrily)
"The Mandarin is a kindly man,
But why is he always late?"

3RD AMB.
"My appointment's for two o'clock
and now it is nearly four."

4TH AMB.
"I am tired of waiting
and I can't wait anymore."

CHORUS	*Repeat Chorus:* He was late, he was late etc.

SERVANTS   If he can't wake up to a chiming clock
Something else will have to be found.
We will hold a competition
For the nicest possible sound.
If you have a sound will you bring it round
To the Mandarin's palace gate.
Any sound you think could wake him,
Bring it round to the palace at eight.

(The clock strikes eight)

DRUMS (play)   ♫♫ ♩ 𝄽 | ♫♫ ♩ 𝄽 |

DRUM
PLAYERS   We bring the sound of drums for the Mandarin.
♫♫ ♩ 𝄽 | ♫♫ ♩ 𝄽 |

That is sure to wake up the Mandarin.
♫♫ ♩ 𝄽 | ♫♫ ♩ 𝄽 |

MANDARIN   "No, no!"

CHORUS   The Mandarin shook his head.

MANDARIN   "Please find something else instead.
That wouldn't get me out of bed."

DRUMS   ♫♫ ♩ 𝄽 | ♫♫ ♩ 𝄽 |

SL. BELLS (play)   ♩ ♩ ♩ ♩ | ♩ ♩ ♩ 𝄽 |

BELL PLAYERS   We bring the sound of bells for the Mandarin.
♩ ♩ ♩ ♩ | ♩ ♩ ♩ 𝄽 |

That is sure to wake up the Mandarin.
♩ ♩ ♩ ♩ | ♩ ♩ ♩ 𝄽 |

MANDARIN   "No, no!"

CHORUS   The Mandarin shook his head.

MANDARIN   "Please find something else instead.
That wouldn't get me out of bed."

SL. BELLS   ♩ ♩ ♩ ♩ | ♩ ♩ ♩ 𝄽 |

CLAVES (play)	♩ ♫ ♩ ♫ | ♩ ♩ ♩ 𝄾 |
CLAVE PLAYERS	We bring the sound of the claves for the Mandarin ♩ ♫ ♩ ♫ | ♩ ♩ ♩ 𝄾 | That is sure to wake up the Mandarin. ♩ ♫ ♩ ♫ | ♩ ♩ ♩ 𝄾 |
MANDARIN	"No, no!"
CHORUS	The Mandarin shook his head.
MANDARIN	"Please find something else instead. That wouldn't get me out of bed."
CLAVES	♩ ♫ ♩ ♫ | ♩ ♩ ♩ 𝄾 |
GIRL	"I would like to sing for the Mandarin, La la la la la la la la la la. Maybe this could wake up the Mandarin. La la la la la la la."
MANDARIN	"That voice is much sweeter than a bird, The loveliest sound I ever heard, So don't find anything else instead, That's just what I need to get me out of bed."
GIRL	"La la la la la la la la la la. La la la la la la la la la la. La la la la la la la la la la. La la la la la la la."
CHORUS	The following morn at break of day, The Mandarin woke up straight away. The girl would sing him the same refrain, The Mandarin never was late again.
AMBS. *(loudly)*	"Has everybody heard?"
ALL	THE MANDARIN IS CURED!
AMBS.	"No longer need we wait."
ALL	THE MANDARIN'S NEVER LATE! He's on time, he's on time, he is right on time Is the good and kindly Mandarin. He's on time, he's on time, he is right on time Is the good and kindly man.

A Little Magic Goes a Wrong Way

Words and Music by
EILEEN DIAMOND

CHORUS

There once was a Wizard, a magical Wizard,
There was nothing he couldn't fix with clever tricks
And lots of magical spells.
He had many lotions and magical potions,
And if you should be standing near,
Some rather funny sounds you'd hear.

WIZARD

"Zip! Bang! Hullabaloo! I'll wave a magic wand or two,
With a swish, swish, swish, I can grant 'most any wish.
Oh Zip! Bang! Hullabaloo! I'll mix a magic spell or two,
It won't take long when I sing this Magical Song."

CHORUS

The Wizard was busy, so busy was he,
He had set up a waiting room with rows of chairs
Where people waited to see
The man with the lotions and magical potions,
And while the people waited there
Some rather funny sounds they'd hear.

WIZARD

"Zip! Bang! Hullabaloo! I'll wave a magic wand or two,
With a swish, swish, swish, I can grant 'most any wish.
Oh Zip! Bang! Hullabaloo! I'll mix a magic spell or two,
It won't take long when I sing this Magical Song."

CHORUS

Because he had so much to do
The Wizard had an assistant too.
He helped to mix the magic brew,
The Wizard taught him spells he knew.

WIZARD
&
ASSISTANT

"Zip! Bang! Hullabaloo! You wave a magic wand or two,
With a swish, swish, swish, you can grant 'most any wish.
Oh Zip! Bang! Hullabaloo! You mix a magic spell or two,
It won't take long when you sing this Magical Song."

CHORUS

Every day when the clock struck four
The Wizard opened up his door,
And people filed in one by one
To ask for something to be done.

BOY
    "Oh please Mister Wizard, my rabbit has gone,
He managed to move the catch and lift the latch,
And now he's out on the run.
I know you do magic, so that's why I'm here,
I've heard you have a magic hat,
And you can make things reappear."

WIZARD
    Well "Zip! Bang! Hullabaloo! I'll see what I can do for you,
With a swish, swish, swish, I can grant 'most any wish.
Oh Zip! Bang! Hullabaloo! I'll mix a magic spell or two,
It won't take long when I sing this Magical Song.
Zip! Bang! Hullabaloo! Zip! Bang! Hullabaloo!
Swish! Swish! Swish!"

BOY
(speaks)
    "Oh thank you Mister Wizard. You really can do magical
things. I'm so pleased to have my rabbit back."

1ST LADY
    "Oh please Mister Wizard, my baby won't grow.
I've tried every recipe and remedy
And still she's terribly slow.
I see you have lotions and magical potions,
Perhaps you have a magic brew,
'Cause I just don't know what to do."

WIZARD
    Well "Zip! Bang! Hullabaloo! I'll see what I can do for you,
With a swish, swish, swish, I can grant 'most any wish.
Oh Zip! Bang! Hullabaloo! I'll mix a magic spell or two,
It won't take long when I sing this Magical Song.
Zip! Bang! Hullabaloo! Zip! Bang! Hullabaloo!
Swish! Swish! Swish!"

1ST LADY
(speaks)
    "Oh Mister Wizard, what a clever magician you are.
Thank you. I'll send all my friends to see you."

CHORUS
    Then one day when the Wizard went
To fetch a new ingredient,
He told his assistant:

WIZARD
    "You carry on and see the people while I'm gone."

2ND LADY
    "Oh please Mister Wizard, this spot on my nose,
I wish it would go away
But every day it grows and grows and grows.
I know you do magic, so that's why I'm here.
I've heard you have a magic wand
And you can make things disappear."

ASSISTANT	"Zap! Bing! Bubble and Stew! I'll see what I can do for you With a swosh! swosh! swosh! Oh my goodness! Oh my gosh! Oh Zap! Bing! Muddle along! I think that something has gone wrong. But it won't take long when I sing the Magical Song. Zap! Bing! Oh what a sight! Bubble and Who? No, that's not right!"
(speaks)	"Oh dear, the Wizard will be angry if he comes back and finds I've done my spelling wrong. I just can't seem to remember the words of the Magical Song."
2ND LADY *(speaks)*	"I don't know what you're up to Mister Wizard, but my spot hasn't gone yet, in fact, it feels as though it's getting bigger! PLEASE can you hurry and make it disappear?"
ASSISTANT *(speaks)*	"Oh er....yes, ummm...Well, the fact is, er... you see.. It has to get bigger before it's banished, but very soon now you will find it's vanished!"
(sings)	"Oh dear, this isn't going well, I can't remember the magic spell. I wonder if someone here can tell? *(Speaks to the audience)* Do YOU know the words of the MAGIC SPELL?" *(Waits for reply from audience, then)* "What's that...? Will you say that a little louder?" *(Waits for response...)* "Oh yes, now I remember..."
(sings)	Zip! Bang! Hullabaloo! You wave a magic wand or two, With a swish, swish, swish, you can grant 'most any wish. Oh Zip! BANG! Hullaballo! You mix a magic spell or two, It won't take long when you sing this Magical Song. Zip! Bang! Hullabaloo! Zip! Bang! Hullabaloo! Swish! Swish! Swish!
2ND LADY *(speaks)*	"Oh Mister Wizard, the spot's not there any more. It's completely gone! Thank you very much, I shall always be grateful to you."

ASSISTANT
(speaks)

"And I shall always grateful to YOU!"
(Holds hand out towards audience)
Thank you."

CHORUS

The assistant had finished, the Wizard returned.

WIZARD

"I hope that you managed everything alright
I was a little concerned."

ASSISTANT

"I must tell you truly, that something went wrong,
But here I have some marvellous friends
Who helped me sing the Magic Song."

WIZARD
&
ASSISTANT

"Zip! Bang! Hullabaloo!
You wave a magic wand or two,
With a swish, swish, swish,
You can grant 'most any wish.
Oh Zip! Bang! Hullabaloo! You mix a magic spell or two,
It won't take long when you sing this Magical Song.
Zip! Bang! Hullabaloo!
Zip! Bang! Hullabaloo!
Swish! Swish! Swish!

Performance CD track listing-CD 1

Backing CD track listing-CD 2

Biographies of performers on CD

Helen Speirs

Helen Speirs is best known as a singer and presenter of shows and music for children. She began her career as co-presenter, with Jonathan Cohen, of the long running BBC Schools Television show *Music Time* and also sang and presented the BBC radio shows *Music Makers, Something To Think About, The Song Tree* and *Listening to Music*. Other recording for children include Eileen Diamond's *Super Songbooks* and *Singing Numbers*. Helen also teaches music in schools and acts as Musical Director for her local theatre drama school. She is thrilled to be involved in another collaboration with Eileen Diamond and Jonathan Cohen in Eileen's Musical Plays.

Jonathan Cohen

Jonathan Cohen won a scholarship to the Royal Academy of Music where he became a Fellow of the Royal College of Organists. Since then he has enjoyed a diverse musical career encompassing performing, composing and conducting symphony orchestras, as well as presenting popular children's programmes – notably *Playschool, Playaway, Hit the Note!* and *Music Time*. He has composed numerous theme tunes and incidental music for children's television programmes, such as *Julia Jekyll and Harriet Hyde* and the ever popular *Come Outside*. He has enjoyed working with Eileen Diamond on many musical projects.

Jonathan has been musical director for many theatre productions including *Side By Side By Sondheim* and *Noel and Gertie* with the actress Patricia Hodge. Since 1995 he has been presenter and conductor of the *Christmas Carol Singalong* at the Royal Albert Hall.